THE RIGHT REPORT
A Practical Guide to Report Writing

Alan Barker

The Industrial Society

First published in 1993 by
The Industrial Society
Robert Hyde House
48 Bryanston Square
London W1H 7LN
Telephone: 0171–262 2401

© The Industrial Society 1993
This edition reprinted 1998, 1999, 2000

ISBN 085290 995 0

1344tw7.00

British Library Cataloguing-in-Publication Data.
A catalogue record for this book is available from the
British Library.

Typeset by: The Midlands Book Typesetting Company, Loughborough
Printed by: Optichrome
Cover design: Rhodes Design

Text illustrations: Sophie Grillet

Contents

CHAPTER ONE: What is a report?
What do reports do?   1
Why do reports fail?   3
Adopting a systematic approach   6

CHAPTER TWO: Preparation
Asking the basic questions   7
Why?   8
Who is the reader?   9
Who is the writer?   12
Where?   13
When?   14

CHAPTER THREE: Gathering material
Facts and opinions   17
Terms of reference   19

Sources of material 20
Sorting material 22
Organizing the material 24
Pattern planning: an example 25

CHAPTER FOUR: Finding a shape
Structuring a report 30
Notation 33
Contents page 33
Page numbers 34
Introduction 35
Findings 36
Conclusions 36
Recommendations 37
Appendices 38
Acknowledgements and glossary 38
References and bibliography 39
Writing a summary 40
Title page 43

CHAPTER FIVE: Accurate, brief and clear
Words and phrases 48
Sentences 52
Sentence analysis: an example 53
Paragraphs 56
Style 56

CHAPTER SIX: Presentation
Layout 61
Illustrations 62
Binding and printing 65

CHAPTER SEVEN: Checking it over

Typing   67
Section revision   69
Checking the first draft   70
The final check   75

Appendices

A: Gunning's fog index   77
B: Writing numbers   81

Bibliography   83

What is a report?

A report is an exercise in persuasion.

The decision-making process within organizations is becoming ever more complex, as managerial responsibilities are distributed more and more widely. More people need to know more of what is going on, so that they can contribute more effectively.

Reports are part of that process. They travel between colleagues; between departments; between managerial levels; or between organizations. They are the means by which detailed knowledge is transmitted to those who need it.

What do reports do?

Reports *define* a subject or problem, and then *gather* relevant facts in order to *present* them as completely and accurately as possible.

But they often do more. The writer *analyses* the facts, and *makes judgements* on them. What the writer *concludes* will form the basis of what action the report *recommends*. The task of the report is to *influence*: to *persuade* the reader that the recommended course of action is the right one.

A report's task, then, is to present a case; and it is precisely when the material is complex, that a report can be the most effective means of communicating it.

A report is not the end of a process, but the beginning of a new one. It is a crucial link in a chain of action. In order to be effective, it must be:

- persuasive
- decisive
- action-centred.

CHECKLIST: Advantages of reports

- A permanent record which can be referred to over time
- Can be duplicated for as many readers as necessary
- Lends its argument – and its writer – authority

- Gives the writer time to organize the material
- Allows the reader time to consider
- Cannot be interrupted
- Adaptable to individual reader
- Transportable – particularly over long distances
- Can act as a powerful advertisement for the organization

Why do reports fail?

More reports are being written than ever before; and yet, in truth, there is not much evidence that they are being read any more than they were in the past.

Writers often resent the time spent on reports. The document will probably not be read; if read, it may not be understood; and it is unlikely to have the desired effect.

At bottom, there may be the sneaking suspicion that we are in some way responsible for this failure. After all, we were employed not to be good writers, but to be good managers.

Often it is our very expertise that is the problem. How do we translate our detailed knowledge of a complex subject into terms the reader will understand? We are confronted with a mountain of material and have no idea where to start.

Why are we writing this document? What should it look like? How should it be structured? What style should it employ? And how to answer these questions with a deadline looming and no time in the day to consider them?

On the other hand, as readers, we have probably all been faced with reports which were uninviting, unattractive and uninformative. Such a report usually assumes that we know far more about its subject than we do. It is full of jargon, unexplained abbreviations, waffle, and high-flown language which is clearly intended to impress but only succeeds in baffling us. It is also interminably long.

The material seems to be in no logical order. There is too little; or, more often, too much. We cannot tell what is important, and what is supporting detail.

From what we can understand, and the lack of page numbers, we suspect that several pages have mysteriously shifted position. It has a title and headings which may be vague, or unintelligible. It may lack headings altogether: information is buried in the unlikeliest places and recommendations are scattered at random.

Spelling, grammar and punctuation are peppered with errors. Occasionally a diagram will appear – incomprehensible, illegible or seemingly unrelated to the text. The typing may be cramped; and the whole report might have been produced on a photocopier which was having a particularly bad day.

We are confused, bored and insulted. The report is consigned to the dustiest corner of the office. It has failed.

CHECKLIST: Why reports fail

WRITER   READER

WRITER	READER
■ Lack of purpose	■ Boring
■ Volume of material	■ Where to start?
■ Lack of confidence	■ Poor spelling
■ No time; deadlines	■ Confused
■ Lack of knowledge of subject	■ Lack of knowledge
	■ Jargon

- Too close to the material
- Not knowing structure
- Where is the information I need?
- What style do I use?
- Complicated information

- No title/headings
- No clear order
- Buried information
- Poor grammar
- Poor illustrations

There are two main reasons why these problems occur:

- The writer is thinking more of the material than the reader. Remember the first golden rule:

Consider the reader.

- The writer is trying to think and write at the same time. This is a recipe for disaster. We must take time to think. The second golden rule is as important as the first:

Separate your thinking from your writing.

Adopting a systematic approach

Report-writing is best tackled systematically. This guide offers a practical approach to each stage in the process of constructing a report:

- Preparation
- Planning
- Structuring
- Writing
- Checking

Such an approach makes writing a challenge rather than a chore. We can be confident at each stage that our efforts are not being wasted, and enjoy the real satisfaction finally of creating an effective report.

What is a report?

CHECKLIST 1

- Advantages of reports:
  - permanent
  - logical
  - authoritative
- Consider the reader
- Separate your thinking from your writing
- A systematic approach:
  - Preparation
  - Planning
  - Structuring
  - Writing
  - Checking

Preparation

Preparation is crucial to the production of any report. Its purpose is to clarify *why*, and *for whom*, we are writing. Above all, it makes clear in our own mind the case we are going to present, and will help us later in deciding how to present it.

Asking the basic questions

The best way to prepare is to ask a series of basic questions.

- Why?
- Who?
- When?
- Where?
- What?
- How?

Asked in this order, the first four of these questions will provoke answers which clarify the last two: *what* material we will need for the report, and *how* we can set about writing it.

7

Why?

What is the purpose of the report?

You may have been asked simply to give a series of facts; but it is much more likely that they are required for a reason.

Try to write that reason down, as a simple verbal phrase.

CHECKLIST: Purposes of reports

- to inform
- to recommend a course of action
- to create understanding
- to present a complete case
- to give the whole picture
- to justify expenditure
- to set out procedures

- to persuade
- to demand action
- to get decisions
- to present opinions
- to co-ordinate tasks
- to pass on progress
- to instruct

From such a phrase, construct a short *statement of objective*, to which you can refer as you write the report.

The *purpose* of the report is not the same as its *subject*.

The subject of an accident report will be the facts: what happened, circumstances, causes, details of damage or injury. The report may, however, have any one of several purposes: to instigate safety procedures, to assess legal liability, or to arrange compensation. It may address some or all of these purposes at once.

The facts remain the same; presentation and emphasis will be determined in each case by the purpose of the report.

If necessary, ask the person commissioning the report exactly what is required. Discuss too how the report will be used: is it to be a consultation document for the Board, a briefing document for use in a meeting, a client report, a manual for use in the workshop? Are there legal implications?

- Agree the purpose of the report
- Define its terms of reference: what areas of information it will cover; what will not be covered
- Write these down and give a copy to both parties

Until you have determined the purpose of the report, you should not proceed.

You should also ask: *Why a report?* Compiling it will be a lengthy and costly exercise: perhaps a presentation, or a series of visits, meetings or interviews, would be more appropriate.

Who is the reader?

We would not speak to an invisible audience; we should not write without having a reader in mind.

The problem, of course, is that a report will very often be read by more than one person; and each will have different requirements.

Reports have *readers* and *users*.

Report readers may be members of senior management, or potential clients. They may or may not have commissioned the report. They may not have much specialist knowledge; but they could well be in control of budgets. They read the whole report, cover to cover. They are, it must be said, rare beasts.

Report users are much more common animals: less ruminative, more restless. They may be colleagues, members of other departments, or specialists with particular needs. We may

know them well; some we may never meet. They may wish to use our report immediately; or it may be months, even years, before they pick it up.

Report users read the summary; then conclusions and recommendations; then turn to the contents page and pick out the various sections they require, in no particular order. There might be parts of our report that they never read at all.

Report readers will appreciate the clarity of our style and the incisiveness of our thought; report users have no time for such niceties. They will want to know what decisions we have reached, what we recommend, and how they are involved. They need to find their way about the report quickly.

How do we accommodate these different needs in one report? We must try to identify the readers and users of our report. Each will have *needs* which the report must aim to satisfy. They may also have *wants* which we cannot satisfy.

All have different levels of knowledge, different expectations, requirements, attitudes, skills, specialisms, even prejudices; as far as possible, all must be borne in mind.

If in doubt: concentrate on the *principal* reader or user. How well do we know them? Are they the decision-maker? How much authority have they got to implement recommendations? Are they a specialist or a 'lay reader'? What are their expectations of the report? What *use* will they make of it?

Our knowledge of the reader will be crucial to the amount and type of research we will undertake, and to the language we will choose in presenting it.

Highly technical or specialized language will confuse and alienate people unfamiliar with it. There is no subject too difficult to be explained to a non-specialist: but our knowledge of the reader will govern how we explain it.

CHECKLIST: The reader

- Reader or user?
- More than one?
- How well known to us?
- Needs/wants?
- Level of authority/status?
- Level of knowledge?
- Specialist or lay person?
- The decision-maker?
- The budget controller?
- What expectations do they have?
- What use will they have for the report?
- Attitudes? Prejudices?
- Confidentiality?

Who is the writer?

You must take responsibility for your report. You are the link between the material and the reader. You will decide how to present the report's case, what information to include (or exclude), how to order it, what language to use, and how to illustrate it. Your name will go on the title page. This is *your* report.

Are you the right person for the job? Do you agree with the purpose of the report? Are you the expert in the subject? Writing the report will certainly *make* you the expert.

Perhaps it is part of your career development to explore the subject under scrutiny. Reports increasingly contribute to academic, vocational or work-related qualifications.

Are you in the right position to write the report? Do you have the right level of knowledge, or access to the information required? Most importantly, do you have the authority to make the recommendations you will wish to make?

Reports are sometimes written by teams or committees. This can work well, if the whole team is involved in establishing the purpose of the report, gathering the information required, agreeing a structure and allocating writers to sections. One team member should be editor of the report, responsible for its final form and wording.

CHECKLIST: The writer

- Your report; take responsibility and claim authority
- Agreement with the purpose of the report?
- The right person?
- The expert?
- The discoverer?
- In a good position within the organization to communicate?
- Level of knowledge?
- Access to information?
- Relationship to readers/users: authority?
- A team or committee: who edits?

Where?

What is the report's destination? Within the department? To another within the organization? To an outside client?

Names and addresses must be exact, and up-to-date. People move from post to post; organizations often have various sites. Companies relocate, expand or 'rationalize'. If the report is going abroad, questions of translation and method of despatch may arise. Time will have to be allocated accordingly.

Where, too, will you write? Is there somewhere quiet and free from interruptions, where work can be done in peace?

Somewhere close to the information you will need to refer to? Some writers have the luxury of a laptop computer, giving them the privilege – perhaps dubious – of being able to work on the train, or at home.

When?

Establish a clear *deadline* – a hand-in date – with the report commissioner: there is nothing more frustrating than rushing a report through to completion, only to find that the reader is on holiday and doesn't need it for another month.

Working back from this date, establish a *schedule*. Keep to it. Allow for all the stages of construction: planning, research, writing, drafting, revising, checking, and proof-reading.

Allow time to gather material. Departments are busy; colleagues can be under pressure; research libraries sometimes have odd opening hours. Information can go out of date quickly, and the updated figures may not yet be available.

Give yourself time, too, to write. Some writers share access to word processors, which can disrupt any attempt at time management. Many a report has been written during the lunch hour. Try to allocate some part of the day as *your* time: when your mind is clearest. It may be at midnight, or very early in the morning. The best work of the day can sometimes be done before breakfast.

CHECKLIST: Where and When

WHERE	**WHEN**
■ Destination	■ Deadline: hand-in date
■ Name/Job title/address/ site/department/room no.	■ Establish schedule:
■ Inside organization/	■ keep to it
■ outside client	■Include latest info.
■ Abroad? Time; translation?	■ May be part of an
■ Method of despatch?	■ ongoing timetable
■ Where to write?	■ Seasonal?
■ Quiet, uninterrupted	■ Allow time to research
■ Close to information	■ Allocate part of each
■ Access to word processor?	■ day to write
■ Working at home?	■ Your best time of day

Only when these four basic questions are answered satisfactorily – *Why? Who? Where? When?* – are you ready to consider the *What?* and the *How?* of writing your report. Leave them unanswered, and you will be in danger of losing your way.

Time spent on these preparatory questions is never wasted. It will be paid off with interest later. The more thorough your preparation, the more efficiently the report will be written, and the more successful it will be in achieving its purpose.

Preparation

CHECKLIST 2

- The basic questions:
  - Why?
- Purpose of the report; why a report; why me?
  - Who?
- Reader or user? Principal reader? Who is the writer?
  - Where?
- Report's destination? Where will it be written?
  - When?
- Deadline? Establish a working schedule: keep to it. Your best time to write?

Gathering Material

We can now ask what material we should be gathering. There may already be a mountain of documents to be tackled; or perhaps there is nothing and we are starting from scratch.

We are faced with a number of important questions:

- Where do I find what I want?
- How much do I need?
- How do I collect it?
- What do I include and leave out – and on what basis?
- What order should it be in?

Facts and opinions

Writing reports involves gathering facts. For some, it seems to consist in virtually nothing else. They are convinced that *everything* should be included, and are terrified that they will

AH SMITHERS! HOW DID THE FACT-FINDING GO?

leave something out. The resulting reports are often admirably complete, but utterly indigestible.

Facts are indeed sacred. It is only on the basis of scrupulously accurate information that the report's conclusions and recommendations can be made. In this respect, all reports should be objective.

Comment, however, is free. You have been *asked* to give your opinions, to come to conclusions and make recommendations. The *choice* of facts, and the *emphasis* placed on some over others, will be governed by the case you are presenting. This is the *subjective* element of the report, and it is as vital as the other, *objective* element. The choices are yours, and yours alone.

Do you know yet what recommendations to make? You may already have a case which the report will be attempting to justify: funding for a research project, for example, or a plan to reorganize a department. Or perhaps you are setting out into the unknown, and you will not know what to recommend until the investigations are complete.

Terms of reference

These – sometimes called the 'scope' or 'parameters' of the report – are the factors influencing the method of research and the nature of the report.

The writer may be asked specifically to consider only one aspect of the subject under scrutiny: the sales figures for the last quarter rather than the last year; the company's operations in this country but not the rest of the world; the procedures in a single department but not the whole orgnaization. The more clearly defined the report's scope, the easier the writer's job will be.

Some terms of reference can be specified without difficulty. Deadlines and budgets can be set. The distribution list should be agreed as early as possible, and matters of confidentiality made clear.

Others are less easy to define. The need for confidentiality may limit the amount of research possible, or suggest particular methods. Ascertaining staff attitudes to a plan submitted by senior management, for example, may prove difficult, and require a careful approach. Evaluating the success of business competitors may be tricky without resort to methods which are unacceptable – or illegal.

Internal politics can actually hamper investigations. Imagine the difficulties faced by a senior police officer investigating allegations of corruption in a neighbouring force. Report writers often face similar problems requiring tact and diplomacy. If we have considered the needs and attitudes of our readers, we should at least now be aware of such difficulties.

CHECKLIST: Terms of reference

- What aspects of the subject?
  - particular geographical area
  - limited period of time
  - part of organization to be studied
  - requirements of a specific client
  - contribution to a discussion/meeting
- Deadline for report: time management
- Available budget
- Distribution list
- Confidentiality
- Internal politics?
- Methods of research possible

Sources of material

Our preparation will have already suggested possible methods of research.

Interviews, questionnaires, team briefings, suggestion boxes, site visits and meetings with clients are common sources of material. Teams will have brainstorming sessions where information and expertise are pooled.

Experiments or technical examination of equipment will result in detailed measurements and calculations. Minutes of meetings give details of previous discussions, decisions, and actions taken. Past reports will yield valuable information – provided, of course, that they have been well written!

Information on clients, or potential clients, can be gleaned from company literature and publicity material. Facts from further afield can be supplied by newspapers, magazines, specialist

journals, periodicals, yearbooks – even telephone directories. Companies exist which disseminate technical and scientific information regularly in journals or on disk.

Other possible sources of information include British Standards, government publications, local authority regulations, dictionaries, technical reference works and encyclopaedias.

Most, if not all, of these can be found in libraries – either local libraries, many of which have excellent reference departments, or national research libraries. Some organizations have their own collections of published and unpublished material.

By far the best way to tackle an unfamiliar library is to ask for help. It is bound to save you time; and there are very few librarians who do not enjoy guiding researchers towards the information they require.

CHECKLIST: Sources of material

Interpersonal
- interviews
- team briefings
- site visits
- brainstorming sessions
- questionnaires
- suggestion boxes
- client meetings

Written: in-house
- experimental results
- minutes of meetings
- technical data
- past reports

Written: commercial
- company literature
- computerized information:
- scientific
- technical
- patents
- publicity material
- catalogues

Library material
- newspapers
- periodicals
- directories
- technical reference books
- government/local govt.
- publications
- books
- theses
- journals
- yearbooks
- dictionaries
- encyclopaedias
- British Standards

- articles

Sorting material

Even the simplest report will include a number of pieces of information, to be gathered over a period of time, however short. All too often this information is simply stuffed in a file, a box, or a bottom drawer, until the evil hour cannot be put off any longer and the writer must retrieve the mound of material and try to make sense of it – hoping that nothing has escaped.

An ideas book keeps a record of the report's material in one place. It also saves time by encouraging preliminary sorting.

It should preferably be A4 size, perhaps turned sideways to give an A3 spread, and hard-backed for durability.

Rule each page into four columns as follows:

Item	Source	Visuals	Category
What do I need?	Where do I find it?	How to illustrate it?	1, 2, 3?
Collect only what is relevant	List for ease of reference aid understanding	Only those which will	Fill in later

As data becomes available, it can be listed in the book, noting in each column the relevant information, its source, ideas for any illustration, and some indication of its importance to the report.

Category 1 material is mainstream information, crucial to the case you are presenting. It will become part of the main text of the report.

Category 2 material is not essential to the report's argument, but will be useful as back-up. It may be necessary for some users, but not others. It may include comprehensive statistics, technical analysis or detailed explanation. This material will probably go into an appendix.

Category 3 material is interesting but of doubtful relevance. You cannot see any place for it in the report at the moment, but are unwilling to dispense with it. It will be put to one side, filed away for future use, or finally discarded.

As your research progresses, material will move between categories. Detailed information in Category 1 may be consigned to an appendix under Category 2. Your hunch that something in Category 3 is actually crucial to your case might result in its being moved to Category 1.

Organizing the material

The time comes when research must end and the construction of the report must begin. It can be difficult to know exactly when this point has arrived: some subjects are seemingly inexhaustible.

You will need to remind yourself, at this stage, of the two basic questions you asked at the beginning:

■ What is the report's purpose?
■ Who is my reader?

You are not merely amassing facts: you are pursuing an argument. You are seeking *conclusions*; you have been asked to make *recommendations*. You cannot move on until you know what these are. Once these are clear in your mind, your research is almost finished.

Your task now is to edit the mass of information you have gathered into a sequence that is logical, decisive and persuasive.

You have a table of items with some indication of categories. You may have assembled the data into sections under rough headings. You might now extract a list of 'keypoints' or 'bullet' points on a separate sheet of paper, drawing arrows between them to achieve some sort of order.

The problem is that lists of this kind have a tendency to become hopelessly complicated, until they are either abandoned or rewritten. Eventually, a list may come out satisfactorily: but by then we will be exhausted, the wastepaper basket will be overflowing, and there will still be the lingering doubt that our thinking is faulty, or that we have left something crucial out.

The reason for these problems is the list itself. Our lives are governed by lists: shopping lists, timetables, catalogues, inventories, lines of management – even action lists and checklists in training manuals! Our education teaches us to make lists; but the fact is that our minds do not easily think in lists.

A list gives material a predetermined order, which automatically gives items at the top an importance they may not deserve. By writing a list, we commit ourselves to a single train of thought. Lists are like tramlines which limit our thinking.

Pattern planning: an example

Pattern plans are an increasingly popular method of organizing information. They allow us to access the vast amount of information in our heads by making associative connections as well as logical ones. They liberate ideas from the tyranny of lists.

To construct a pattern plan, draw a circle in the middle of a piece of paper – preferably unlined, or turned through 90° so that you are not tempted to write sentences or lists.

Write the purpose of the report in the circle, or draw a picture or symbol which represents it.

Write down any ideas connected with the report's purpose that suggest themselves to you. Write down ideas as they come: in no particular order. Draw pictures or symbols as memory joggers. Omit nothing, however trivial! It is essential that no ideas are 'edited out'.

Highlight 'key' ideas, in any order. As you become acquainted with pattern plans, these will tend to be the first to emerge. Use a different colour for each key idea, and write in capitals so that they stand out.

Group pieces of information under each key idea, connecting them by 'branches' and 'twigs'. Some items will have to move in order to find their proper group.

Add more information to each heading s it occurs to you. Keep the pattern plan in a prominent position, reviewing it regularly, adding, deleting and moving information until you are satisfied that it is complete.

Assign an order to the key points. The order will depend on the nature both of the report, and of your recommendations. It may suggest itself to you as you pattern plan. The information may be ordered in various ways:

- advantages/disadvantages
- old system/new system
- chronologically
- cause and effect
- cost benefits

All of this may at first seem like aimless daydreaming. In fact, daydreaming is one of the most creative forms of thinking. Pattern plans harness our creativity and link it to our powers of logic.

They can be used in any situation requiring the gathering and ordering of information. You can use them at every stage of writing a report to clarify your thoughts. They have a number of advantages as thinking tools:

- rapidity: we can think freely putting ideas on the page more quickly;
- completeness: we can see the whole at a glance and are less likely to omit something by mistake;
- efficiency: they gather the material and order it *simultaneously*.

Most importantly, pattern plans are *individual*. We all think differently, making connections between ideas according to our

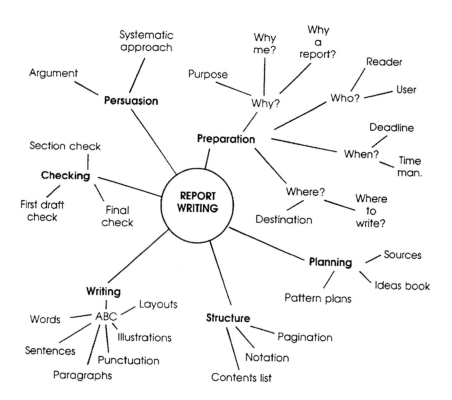

needs, taste and experience. Don't worry, then, if your finished plan looks a mess. You know what it means; and anyway, the messy ones are usually the best! Material in a pattern plan will make sense to us, and so have a far better chance of making sense to our reader.

Each highlighted, key idea on the pattern plan will form the basis of a section of the final report. You can take each key idea and pattern plan it alone, ordering the material into groups that will form the basis of sub-sections.

You are now in a position to delve into as much detail as time allows, including what is relevant, assigning inessential information to appendices, and rejecting what is necessary: secure in the knowledge that the shape of your thinking is correct, and that the heart of the report will be well-structured. Above all, your material will be governed by an overall plan that reflects the argument *you* want to present.

Gathering material

CHECKLIST 3

- Facts are sacred; comment is free. A report needs both
- Define your terms of reference
- Use every relevant source of information
- Ideas book to record research
- Pattern plan the material required
- Put the information in order, according to purpose of report and nature of recommendations

---

Finding a Shape

Our pattern plan includes a number of key ideas, with information gathered under each one. The key ideas, as section headings, have been assigned an order. The report is beginning to take shape.

However: this is *not* yet the time to begin writing!

No self-respecting house-builder would start laying bricks before being given a detailed architect's drawing. Similarly, beware of putting pen to paper – or fingers to keyboard – until you have drawn up a detailed structure of your report: in other words, a contents list.

Establishing a list of contents before beginning to write has a number of advantages:

- Clarifying your thinking: you can see everything at a glance and note omissions or repetitions
- Flexibility: it is far easier to move headings around on a single page, than long sections of text

- The plan can be checked quickly by a colleague to confirm the logic of your argument
- The writing, when you come to it, will be quicker and easier
- You can write the individual sections of the report in any order
- You have the satisfaction, at this stage, of seeing the report take shape before your eyes on one sheet of paper

It is essential to think in terms of *sections*: they are the framework into which the information will be fitted, like rooms in the house which in time will be furnished. Without clearly defined sections, the report will lack cohesion, and the shape of your argument will be obscured by incidental or irrelevant detail.

A typical list might look, at this stage, something like this:

BACKGROUND: Terms of reference; identify problem
PAST RESEARCH: others; mine
PRESENT RESEARCH: UK; Europe (site reports; interviews)
FINDINGS: statistics; key factors
POSSIBLE SOLUTIONS: cost constraints; optimum solution

Headings are very vague and sub-headings may not yet be in the right order ('identify problem' might usefully precede 'terms of reference', for instance): but the overall structure of the report is becoming clear. The main headings will eventually be the sections of the report, and the sub-headings the sub-sections. We have the beginnings of a contents list.

Structuring a report

Some reports are produced on prepared forms: visit reports and site reports, for example. You may be contributing to a series

THE CORONER HAS CHOSEN
TO SUBMIT HIS REPORT IN
PULP NOVEL FORM, M'LUD

of reports which are produced in a standard format (perhaps on a regular basis). Readers, users or clients may be expecting a report structure consistent with what they have received before. It would be perverse and inappropriate in any of these cases to break with convention.

Scientific, laboratory or technical reports follow clear structural conventions. Academic departments may make specific structural requirements of long essays or theses.

Past practice can be useful in suggesting what structure to adopt. Companies sometimes have established procedures for the layout and structure of reports: if not written down, at least evident in the ways in which past reports have been written.

Copying slavishly, however, can compound bad habits. Adopt a critical stance to past work and seek to improve on it where possible.

Most formal business reports will follow a similar structure.

CHECKLIST: Structure of a report

- Title page
- Acknowledgements
- Summary
- Contents page
- Introduction
- Findings
- Conclusions
- Recommendations
- Appendices
- References
- Bibliography
- Index

Headings should be reviewed regularly so that they are as *specific* as possible, reflecting accurately the material within each section.

- *Are they accurate?* Do they cover all the sub-headings gathered under them?
- *Are they brief?* No more than three or four words.
- *Are they clear?* "Introduction" and "Findings", for example, may not mean much to your reader.
- Do they follow the sequence set out in the Checklist? Recommendations, for example, must follow Conclusions.
- Are the sub-headings clear? And in logical order within each section?
- Is there a gap in the logical progression of ideas? A section may be missing.
- Too many sub-headings in one section? Perhaps the main heading is too vague and the material should be split into several sections.

- Is a section too short? It might be amalgamated with another, or be placed elsewhere as a sub-section.
- Do you have material for every section and sub-section? More research may be needed.
- Is every section necessary? Perhaps one or two are redundant and can be discarded.

Notation

All reports should be notated: each section and sub-section should be numbered.

Decimal numbering is generally recognized to be the most straightforward method of notation. It shows more clearly than any other the hierarchy of your thoughts.

Section	1
Sub-section	1.1
Paragraph	1.1.1
	1.1.2
Sub-section	**1.2**

Three sub-divisions should prove quite sufficient: if you run to four or more, you risk confusing your reader. Rethink the structure of the section.

Every section of the report should be notated in this way, apart from the contents page itself and the summary, which will not be notated; and any Appendices, which are usually identified by capital letters and numbers.

Contents page

Any report worthy of the name should have a contents list. It acts as a guide to readers of the shape of the report, and as a map for users to find the information they require.

For these reasons, it should include the title of every section and sub-section of the report – including Appendices. A separate list of illustrations is advisable where a large number are included.

For a report of three pages or more, it is worth putting the contents list on a separate page.

CHECKLIST: Layout of a contents page

1. PROPOSED GARDEN DESIGN 00
   1.1 Preparation 00
   1.1.1 Survey of plot 00
   1.1.2. Consultation with owner 00
   1.1.3. Budget constraints 00

1.2 Planning 00
   1.2.1 Existing features 00
   1.2.2 New features 00
   1.2.3 Construction materials 00

etc.

Page numbers

These obviously cannot be entered on the contents page at this stage, although it is a good idea to number the pages of the report as you write it.

It is common practice to leave the title page unnumbered, and to number every other page before the Introduction with roman numbers (*I, ii, iii, iv* . . .) If you choose to number the preliminary pages in this manner, try not to run to more than five or six (*v* or *vi*).

The best way of paginating is to number pages within each section. Section 1, for example, might run from page 1/1 to 1/5, Section 2 from 2/1 to 2/13, and so on. Numbering by sections is of great help to typists – particularly if loose sheets fall out of order – and reduces the need for constant renumbering as the report grows in size. Additions ('2/5a') and deletions ('No page 1/3') are easily indicated in manuscript or first draft without affecting the pagination of other sections.

Appendices are numbered in the same way, but with letters instead of numbers: A/1, A/2 and so on.

Now – at last! – we are ready to begin writing. Thanks to our detailed contents list, we can start anywhere in the report, and work on sections in any order. Some sections must clearly wait: we cannot summarize a report we have not yet completed, for example; and the title may need time to acquire the punchy, attractive form we will need.

Introduction

This includes:

- Terms of reference
- Background: how it came about; who commissioned it
- Objectives: purpose, intended uses of the report
- Methods: of investigation, analysis
- Arrangement of information

The amount of introduction required will depend on the reader's or user's knowledge. What *needs* to be explained? What can be taken for granted? Too much can be boring; too little will create confusion.

Findings

Or 'body', or 'discussion'. Here is the evidence: the facts dug up by the research. Opinions, conclusions and recommendations must be excluded from this section.

All this material is ready sorted and arranged. Your task now is to present it *persuasively*. Language, layout and illustrations will all contribute to convincing your reader of the relevance of the facts you are giving.

When material is complicated or excessively detailed, try to extract the points crucial to your argument, putting statistics, diagrams or other data into an appendix.

Conclusions

The order of your conclusions should follow the order of the findings.

Conclusions are an assessment of the facts: your considered opinion based on your analysis of the evidence. Never introduce new evidence at this stage. If the research is sound, you should have no fear of stating your conclusions unambiguously.

An accident report might conclude:

- *There is a faulty light fitting in the stairwell.*
- *The staircarpet is loose and threadbare in places.*
- *The angles of the stairwell make traffic of heavy goods impractical.*

Recommendations

This is the most important part of the report. Your conclusions have identified the problems: the recommendations will suggest courses of action to resolve them.

Recommendations should be specific, measurable and achievable. Be sure to allocate responsibility for the actions you recommend. Give names and deadlines.

Our accident report's recommendations, based on the conclusions we have come to, might be:

- *House manager to replace light fitting in the stairwell.*
- *Operations room to order a new staircarpet urgently.*
- *Memo to all delivery staff to use Entrance D in future.*

The manner in which you make your recommendations is crucial to their effectiveness. Do not hedge: state your preferred course of action clearly and directly. Advise, urge, suggest: you want to convince your readers, not alienate them.

If there is a range of possible options, make the fact clear without seeming to sit on the fence. *Somebody* will have to choose one course of action over the others: allocate the responsibility of choice to the appropriate person. Do not be afraid to suggest a preferred option. You, after all, are now the expert.

Remember that you are responsible for the recommendations you make. You must be prepared to accept that responsibility.

Appendices

Appendices are ideal if your report is aimed at a mixed audience: particularly of technical and non-technical readers.

They contain Category 2 material (see Chapter 3, 'Gathering material'): information not essential to your argument, but which proves your case. Here, too, is the detailed material required by some specialist users or future decision-makers.

Statistics, diagrams (perhaps on fold-outs for ease of use with the main text), charts, graphs, computer print-outs, extracts from magazines or newspapers, glossaries and lists of abbreviations: all may find their way into an appendix.

Appendices are usually given letters rather than numbers, to indicate that they are not part of the main report. They might be printed on differently coloured paper for easy reference. Sub-division can be effected with decimal notation: A.1, A.2, and so on – but this is rarely necessary. Remember to include them in the contents page and page numbering.

Acknowledgements and glossary

These might be placed either at the beginning of the report or at the end. Acknowledgements acting as PR – thanking a number of companies for their participation and sponsorship, for example – are certainly best placed prominently at the head of the report. A glossary too can be a welcome sight early in the document. Alternatively, if neither section is this important, they are best placed at the end. Be sure to include them in the contents list.

References and bibliography

These are lists of material, published or unpublished, which you have consulted in the preparation of the report. References usually precede the bibliography.

Sources of material for these lists include:

- Books
- Periodicals
- Published reports
- In-house reports
- Minutes of meetings
- Proceedings of conferences
- Theses, published or unpublished

References are to material specifically referred to, or quoted, in the text of the report. At the point in the text where the reference is made, it is marked with a number, perhaps in square brackets:

Recent research in the US [3] has indicated . . .

The reference list is best placed at the end of the report. References will be listed in the order in which they occur, and numbered sequentially.

Each reference should include all the information needed to retrieve the original material. A typical reference (in this case fictitious) will be laid out as follows:

> 3. *Danby, P.H.,* **Modern Gardens,** *New York, 1989, p.254.*
>
> [Author; title; place and date page of publication; ref.]

Take care in references to periodicals to include the title of the article, and details of the periodical number and date:

> 25.Danby, P.H., 'The use of water in the garden', Garden Design, Vol. 46, Jan. 90, pp.45–52.

The *Bibliography* lists material not referred to in the report, but which you may have used in research, or which will be of interest to the report reader or user. Items in the bibliography are laid out exactly similarly to references, but are listed alphabetically by name of author or organization, and unnumbered.

Begin these lists – on record cards or in a file on disk – as soon as it becomes clear that you will need them. Nothing is more tedious than assembling such material after writing a long report, and much time can be wasted searching frantically for a reference that has been forgotten or gone astray.

Writing a summary

The summary is one of the most important elements of any report, and can be the most difficult to write.

For the first-time reader, the summary gives an overall view of what the report is about. For other readers and users, it serves as a reminder, perhaps prior to a meeting where the report will be discussed; or as an indication of how the sections relevant to them fit into the report as a whole.

Summaries are beginning to take on an increasingly independent role. They will be read by – or at least circulated to – people who may have a general interest in the report but have no time (or inclination) to read it: including senior management, who need an overall view of what decisions have been taken, or are being suggested, in the department or organization. Decision-makers and action-takers may look only to the summary to tell them what to do. Research suggests that the vast majority of managers only ever read the summaries of reports.

For these reasons, summaries are sometimes split into general or *management summaries*, and *executive summaries*, stressing recommendations and actions.

The summary must be as action-centred as the rest of the report. It should also explain the report's background sufficiently to anybody who will not be reading the whole document.

Because it often circulates independently of the rest of the report, the summary page should include:

■ Report title and author
■ Date
■ Reference number or code
■ Any indication of confidentiality

The summary is obviously the final section of the report to be written. It must be impressive. Like the blurb on the flyleaf or back cover of a book, this short statement will sell the report to its readers.

The material in the summary need not – indeed, probably will not – follow the order of the report itself. The emphasis must be on results rather than method, on recommendations rather than research.

Tackle the task systematically. Do not leave the writing of the summary to the last ten minutes!

■ Decide what is important

If you were forced to reduce your report to half a page, what would you most want to save?

Write these essential points in a few sentences, emphasizing conclusions, recommendations, and action points.

■ Background

What does the reader need to know in order to understand the context of these few points? Remember that the summary should be able to stand on its own. Include too much rather than too little: cutting is far easier than adding later.

■ Link the two sections into prose

Use paragraphs and layout to emphasize the most important or urgent points.

There is no need to restrict yourself to one paragraph, if two or three are more helpful.

■ Check and reduce

By now the summary should be accurate, unambiguous, and too long.

Cut out:

Repetition
Lists
Inessential detail
Unnecessary jargon
Examples
**Figures except where absolutely necessary (in
    recommendations, perhaps)**

Cut down your language: hunt out wordy expressions, unnecessary phrases and convoluted sentences. Be aware that in cutting material down, there is a great danger of creating sentences which are too long.

Ask a colleague to read your final version. Does it make sense as a separate item? Is anything missing?

Title page

At last the report is nearing completion. All that remains is a title page.

Any but the very shortest reports should have a separate title page, informing, interesting and inviting its potential readers. First impressions are of immense importance: a report with a crowded, badly presented or boring title page will begin to fail before it has even been opened.

You may be guided by company convention in the matter of covering and titling reports. Normally, the title page will include:

- Title, centred and a third of the way down the page: the biggest and boldest element
- Author's name or names
- Date
- Reference number
- Receiver's name or signature
- Company name, address, or logo where appropriate
- Confidentiality mark
- Copy number (for restricted reports)

A distribution list can make the title page look untidy. It may be better to give it a page to itself.

Give thought to the title. It should be precise: a vague or ambiguous title can cause immediate confusion. "Communication Breakdowns", for example, might refer to telecommunication systems, team briefing, or an incident on the railway. "Business Review" is so vague as to be almost useless.

The title should also be short: "Long-term strategic plans for service and product diversification" hardly whets the appetite! A 'punchy' title stays in the mind and sells the report; it can also help to identify it, particularly in a file on computer where documents are listed by keywords.

Balancing these two requirements can be tricky. A stylist solution – much in favour with academic writers and HMSO – is to give the report a short main title followed by a longer, more explanatory sub-title. Our "Business Review" might attract a lot more readers if it were entitled:

BIGGER AND BETTER

A strategy for growth

The title, together with the summary and contents page, acts as an invitation to our readers to enter the world of the report. All three are summaries, in fact, guiding the reader's mind into the argument, and preparing them for the material we are about to present.

Finding a shape

CHECKLIST 4

- Draw up a contents list
- Adapt to a formal report structure
- Headings: accurate, brief and clear
- Decimal notation for sections
- Number all pages
- Summary:
  - emphasize conclusions, recommendations and actions
  - brief statement of background to the report
- Title: precise but punchy

5

Accurate, Brief and Clear

Reports should communicate, not mystify. Language should not be used to impress: it should create understanding. Reports are meant to be read and used: not to be studied.

There is no such thing as 'business English': there is only good English. Beware of writing in a certain way because it seems more 'businesslike' or 'correct'. Be guided by the first preparatory questions you asked yourself:

- The purpose of the report;
- The needs of the reader.

Review what you have thought and discovered up to now, and try to put those thoughts and facts down on paper with language that is *accurate, brief* and *clear*.

Words and phrases

Accuracy means using the right word for the right job. Remember that words can change their meaning according to their context. 'Viable' to an economist might mean 'profitable'; to a gynaecologist it will refer to the ability of a foetus to live outside the womb. The words we choose will depend crucially on our readers: on their level of understanding, and their relationship with us.

Language also changes over time. Words lose meanings and acquire new ones. Changes in technology or working practices can create new vocabularies. A *disc* in the 1960s was something very different from a *disk* in the 1990s. Words appropriate in a report thirty years ago may now be old-fashioned.

All professions or business communities have words (and abbreviations) which have a specific and limited meaning within that community. To an outsider, the words are meaningless: they are *jargon*.

HE'S SPENT THE MORNING DIGESTING ALEX'S PROSE

Jargon has its place. A report circulating only among fellow experts can quite properly use specialized terminology to provide clearer and quicker communication. If readers are non-specialists, however, jargon should be kept to a minimum. Explanations of technical terms should always be provided – either as they appear, or in a glossary.

There are other kinds of private language in business: *'buzz words'* used between colleagues (and competitors!) to suggest status, the latest fashion, membership of the clique. All too often they create nothing but confusion, annoyance, and antagonism. They have no place in any report.

Brevity is the soul not only of wit, but also of understanding. Use the short word rather than the long one. Do not 'endeavour to ascertain': try to find out. Why 'utilise' when you can use, or 'facilitate' when you can make easier?

Sometimes whole phrases can be dispensed with. The word *cliché* derives from printing: originally it was the metal stereotype from which an engraving was printed. Now it refers to stereotyped phrases, words which go about glued together in blocks, clogging the language. *Each and every one of us* is guilty of using clichés in the *normal course of events*, particularly *in view of the fact that, in this day and age, the vast majority of people* are under *tremendous pressure* to get *cast-iron, copper-bottomed* results, if not as soon as *humanly* possible, then certainly *in the fullness of time*.

Clichés are a form of automatic writing: they betray a lack of thinking. They have a habit of spreading like weeds: constant attention is needed if they are to be rooted out.

Tautology is another enemy to brevity. Why say the same thing twice?

red in <u>colour</u>
a <u>joint</u> collaboration
the <u>true</u> facts
in <u>close</u> proximity

All the words underlined here are unnecessary repetitions that add nothing to the sense of the phrase.

Tautologies can be difficult to spot, and often arise through a concern for formality.

'The reason is because . . .' is a common tautology in reports, usually arising in long sentences:

The reason the machine broke down and had to be repaired on this occasion, as on others, was because the operator had failed to check it beforehand.

The writer has forgotten 'The reason' and so brought in 'because'. Correctly, the sentence should read:

The reason the machine broke down . . . was that the operator . . .
– or:
The machine broke down . . . because the operator . . .

Clarity is a matter of leaving no room for ambiguity or wrong assumptions. You must know the facts, and state them precisely.

Empty phrases like *in the region of, in the area of, around about, or a certain amount of,* arouse suspicion: is the writer covering up something unpleasant, or simply masking ignorance?

Loaded words carry overtones which may or may not be intended. During a staff survey, a person may have been *approached, asked a question, questioned, interviewed,* or even *interrogated*: the implications of the manner in which they have been treated will differ in each case.

Perhaps the greatest threat to clarity in reports comes from *abstract words*. Concepts are far less easy to grasp than concrete, descriptive words or examples, which the reader can visualize.

Be specific. Break a complicated explanation into its constituent parts. This is particularly true when dealing with processes or procedures.

Satisfaction *of these levels of* evaluation *within each stock management* procedure *should, in principle, be sufficient for* acceptability *but, if* excellence *is to be achieved, the* expectation *must be that suitable* provisions *are made to increase internal storage* security.

All the italicised words in this sentence are abstract: it would be hard to judge from them that the sentence is about installing burglar alarms.

It should be sufficient to check stock in the way we recommend at each stage of its journey through the warehouse. The best course of action, however, would be to install security systems in the warehouse.

This version splits the two main ideas into two sentences, and replaces all the abstract words with concrete ones. As far as possible, the language in any report should be like this second version: *specific, descriptive, and action-centred.*

CHECKLIST: Watch your language!

- ■ Accurate: Jargon/technical words
  New words
  Words with new meanings
  Buzz words: in-house or professional
  terminology

■ Brief: Short words instead of long ones
                        Clichés
                        Tautology (the reason is because)
                        Language to impress
■ Clear: Ambiguous words
                        Empty words
                        Loaded words
                        Abstract words

Sentences

Short sentences are easier to read than long ones. We are trained, when reading, to stop and absorb information fully only when we come to a full stop. If we cannot stop and absorb, we must go on, 'mopping up' whatever we can, until finally we are forced to give up and take another run at the sentence.

Use your shortest sentences in prominent positions: to head paragraphs or sections.

The strongest positions in any sentence are the beginning and the end. The most important ideas – the 'key' words – are best placed in these strong positions.

Ideas can often find themselves isolated within sentences. The connections between them – association, logical progression, or contrast – should be expressed by link words or phrases, and by punctuation, which direct the reader's thinking and encourage him or her to continue.

Link words and phrases include:

■ In addition
■ In contrast to
■ On the other hand

- At the same time
- Bearing in mind
- Nevertheless
- As a result
- However

But, and, therefore and *also* are powerful linking words, but should not, as a rule, begin a sentence.

Tautology can afflict sentences as well as words. Writers sometimes feel that an important idea must be stated twice if it is to make its effect. Not so. The bigger the idea, the more simply it must be expressed.

Sentences grow out of control when we try to cram too many ideas into them. We are thinking and writing at the same time. The only answer is to separate thought from writing.

Sentence analysis: an example

Any sentence of 25 words or more should be analysed and reconstructed. This can be done simply by cutting out clichés, redundant or vague words, tautologies and so on. Alternatively, we can use a 4-point plan:

1. List the ideas in the sentence, reordering if necessary to make logical sense.
2. Rewrite each idea as a separate sentence.
3. Connect into prose, using link words or phrases or punctuation if necessary.
4. Check language for accuracy, brevity and clarity.

This sentence, from a real report, urgently needs to be rewritten:

The committee had agreed to consider three major venues, Hartlepool, Birmingham, and Leeds, although Windermere

was examined as a possible venue it was considered to be too far west and too removed from the industry to be able to accommodate the conference successfully, and the results of their deliberations are communicated in Appendix C, page 46, which indicates that a decision was made in favour of Leeds as the setting for the 1994 conference.

There is no one way to do this! A possible solution might be as follows:

1. *Ideas in the sentence:*
a. Four 1994 conference venues: Hartlepool, Birmingham, Leeds, Windermere.
b. Windermere discounted: too far from the industry, too far west.
c. Leeds the venue chosen.
d. Results in Appendix C, page 46.
2. *Rewrite each idea as a separate sentence:*
a. The committee considered four possible venues for the 1994 conference: Hartlepool, Birmingham, Leeds, and Windermere.
b. Windermere was discounted immediately, on account of its being too far west and too far removed from the industry.
c. After due deliberation, Leeds was chosen as the venue.
d. The full results of this research are given in Appendix C, page 46.
3. *Connect into prose, using links as necessary:*
The committee considered four possible venues for the 1994 conference: Hartlepool, Birmingham, Leeds, and Windermere. However, Windermere was discounted immediately, on account of its being too far west and too far removed from the industry. Finally, after due deliberation, Leeds was chosen as the venue. The full results of this research are given in Appendix C, page 46.

4. *Check language for accuracy, brevity, clarity:*
- *On account of its being, after due deliberation* are clichés.
- *Leeds* should be more prominent in the sentence.
- The appendix information could be separated out.
- Is *However* necessary?

The final version reads:

The committee considered four possible venues for the 1994 conference: Hartlepool, Birmingham, Leeds and Windermere. Windermere was discounted immediately: it is too far west, and too isolated from the industry. Finally, after much thought, we decided upon Leeds.

The details of our research are in Appendix C, page 46.

Such analysis may seem time-consuming at first, but with practice it will become second nature; and if it saves the annoyance of explanatory telephone calls later, it is worth the trouble.

CHECKLIST: Sentences

- Short easier to read than long
- Should vary in length
- None longer than 25 words
- Big idea: short sentence
- Introduction of idea or section: short sentence
- Summary of idea or section: short sentence
- Strong places in sentence: beginning and end
- Connect sentences with link words and punctuation

- Long sentence (more than 25 words)?
    - list ideas, reordering for sense
    - rewrite each idea as a separate sentence

> – connect into prose, using link words or phrases or punctuation
> – check language for accuracy, brevity and clarity

Paragraphs

Paragraphs present information on one aspect of a subject. They may have more than one sentence; they will only ever have one theme.

Paragraphs, like headings, are signposts, guiding the reader's eye through the material. Short paragraphs at the head of each section can summarize the theme of the section as a whole. Subsequent paragraphs will contain only one idea or detail of the main theme.

The first, short sentence of each paragraph should summarize the paragraph. The reader can then pick up from these *topic sentences* the gist of the paragraph as a whole.

Use link words at the beginning of each paragraph to guide the reader from one idea to the next.

CHECKLIST: Paragraphs

- Usually more than one sentence: only one theme
- Short topic paragraph at beginning of section
- Short summary sentence at beginning of each paragraph
- Connect paragraphs with link words and phrases

Style

"Proper words in proper places make the true definition of style," wrote Jonathan Swift. But what is 'proper'?

Reports are so often returned to their writers marked: "Poor style" or "Not company style"; but if the writer dares to ask what 'good style' or 'company style' is, the answer is usually: "Well, not this."

To be fair, some organizations do produce writing manuals or guidelines; but many report writers still labour under the burden of a 'company style' which is no more than an excuse for waffle and pomposity.

Reports are formal documents. They are not personal communications (unlike memos or letters): a certain formality of expression is appropriate. This does not mean that the language of a report should be unnatural; but it should not draw attention to itself.

Slang, colloquialisms, and metaphors (especially mixed ones), are to be avoided; as are jokes (although humour can have its place in the most serious report) and foreign words used for effect. Abbreviations should be employed sparingly, and their meanings listed in a prominent place, "e.g." and "i.e." can be used to introduce lists of items, but in a block of prose, the words in full are neater.

Central to a report's style is the question of the person in which it is written. Many writers feel that reports are objective and should therefore be impersonal.

It was discovered on this occasion that . . .
The measurements were taken . . .
Readings were obtained from five sub-stations . . .

This use of the impersonal, *passive voice* complicates the language of the report, introducing convoluted constructions and overlong sentences. It also fails to allocate responsibility for the actions described.

If the writer has produced the report alone, and has the authority to make recommendations, that responsibility should be reflected in the language of the report. This does not mean using 'I' continually; it *does* mean using the *active voice* wherever possible.

I discovered on this occasion that . . .
The measurements showed . . .
Five sub-stations supplied readings . . .

Remember that impersonal statements can create meanings you may not intend. *I do not believe* is substantially different from *It is not to be believed*.

Most importantly, do not be afraid to say:

I recommend that . . .

This is *your* report: let it say so on every page!

Beware, too, of "we", "our" and "us": to whom do they refer? If the report has been produced by a team, on behalf of a company – for an external client, perhaps – or speaks for a profession, the report should say so:

The team worked for several weeks . . .
The department has regularly reviewed . . .
The company believes . . .
Architects have found over the past ten years that . . .

Mistakes in spelling, grammar or punctuation will clearly detract from good style. All writers should have on their desks:

- A good dictionary
- A thesaurus
- A guide to written English

Examples of these will be found in the bibliography.

Style is personal. It cannot be acquired and put on, like a coat; it must be nurtured. Practise the skills of choosing words, constructing sentences, and building paragraphs, whenever you have the chance: jotting down a memo, penning a letter. They will become habitual.

Beware of blind imitation: find the mode of expression which is appropriate to you. Welcome help, but resist imposed alterations. Nobody is more useful that a trusted colleague who can give unbiased suggested and practical examples; the manager who wields a red pen without explanation should be challenged.

A good writer feeds on other writing: other reports, literature produced by the organization; magazines, books, letters in the local newspaper. Read whatever interests you; try to read every day. You will begin to notice when something is well-written, and that critical sense will pass into your own writing.

CHECKLIST: Enemies to good style

- Pompous language
- Metaphors (especially mixed ones!)
- Foreign phrases used for effect
- Clichés
- Slang
- Jokes (though humour can be useful)
- Colloquialisms
- Abbreviations (e.g., i.e.)
- The passive voice (it was discovered . . .)
- Responsibility not indicated (especially conclusions and recommendations)
- Mistakes in grammar, spelling, punctuation
- Imitation of other styles

Accurate, brief and clear

CHECKLIST 5

- Words
  - short words not long ones
  - avoid jargon; buzz words; clichés, tautology; ambiguous words; empty words
  - concrete not abstract
- Sentences
  - big idea: short sentence
  - key words at beginning and end of sentence
  - rewrite sentences over 25 words long
- Paragraphs
  - short topic sentence at beginning
  - summary paragraph at head of section
- Style
  - Formal but not pompous
  - Straightforward but not colloquial
  - Check spelling, grammar, punctuation
  - Don't imitate

Presentation

The first impression your reader will have of your report is the look of the thing. No matter how accurately, briefly and clearly it is written, a report poorly presented has little chance of being read. Layout, illustrations, the use of typeface, emphasis, and even binding, are all invitations to your reader.

Layout

Layout displays the shape of your thoughts. Above all, it should be *consistent* throughout the report.

Make sure that the text follows the notation on your contents page, and that the notation is clearly displayed throughout. Begin each new section on a new page; indent sub-sections.

Emphasize main headings and sub-headings by giving them plenty of space and using whatever printing devices are available: capitals, bold type, underlining, or italics.

The use of space on the page is crucial. Use wide margins to ensure that none of the text is in danger of disappearing into a binding or having holes punched through it. Take particular care if printing on two sides of the paper.

Double spacing will help to dispel the danger of a clogged page. Right justification, though far easier to achieve on word processors than typewriters, is still less popular than a 'ragged' right edge, which is considered more attractive to read.

Any itemized information should be presented as a list, laid out vertically, emphasized with stars or 'bullets', and surrounded with space. Lists are immensely useful in breaking up a page and providing emphasis.

CHECKLIST: Layout

- Consistency of layout throughout report
- Notation consistent with contents page
- Display section numbers and page numbers clearly
- Number pages throughout
- New page for each section
- Indent sub-sections
- Emphasize headings and sub-headings
- Wide margins
- Double spacing
- Avoid right justification
- Use lists as much as possible

Illustrations

A picture can be worth a thousand words: A good illustration presents complex information briefly, and can summarize an important point. It must be relevant and useful: if it is not *essential* to the argument of the report, it should not be used.

All illustrations should be referred to in the text. The common practice in reports is to refer to *all* forms of illustration – diagrams, graphs, tables, pie charts, bar charts, pictograms, photographs, drawings, maps and plans – as *Figures*. They should be labelled with a title and a decimal number. Thus **Figure 5.1** is the first in section 5: **Figure B.1** is the first in Appendix B. A list of Figures might even be appended to the contents list.

Figures should be in a form familiar to the reader, and easy to produce. Above all, they should be *simple*. The point made by the illustration should be clear almost at a glance.

Use very few words in illustrations: only title, labels, scales, numbers and other essential information. Words should be printed or typed, not handwritten. Do not be tempted to add arrows or comments. The illustration itself should do the job.

Illustrations should appear where they are needed: on the page where they are referred to. A turn of the page, even only overleaf, will result in split attention. The picture will automatically take precedence, and the text will not be read accurately, at least on first reading.

On the other hand, a paragraph should never be split for an illustration. Introduce the picture: present it: and then discuss it.

If the discussion will take several pages – or if you are going to refer to it at various points throughout the report – use a *fold-out*. It should be placed after the last reference in the text, for obvious reasons: probably as an appendix.

Illustrations are best presented in landscape format: the horizontal edge longer than the vertical. Try to achieve this without the necessity of turning the page. If the document *must* be turned through 90°, it should be clockwise. Margins should be as wide as, if not wider than, for text.

Photographs, regulations, computer print-outs, newspaper cuttings or pages from other publications, are sometimes included in reports, often with little regard for the quality of their reproduction. Material that will not copy successfully should either be reproduced in another way, or omitted. Take great care with photographs; estate agents are not alone in sometimes producing foggy pictures which are worse than useless.

Pages filled only with illustrations must still be numbered; and there should be space below the illustration for its title and number.

Finally: remember that you must abide by the law of copyright. Do not assume that an in-house report will get away with reproducing material without permission. Once copied and distributed, material can find itself in unexpected places.

CHECKLIST: Illustrations

- Relevant, useful, essential to argument
- Main text or Appendix?
- Simplicity: information at a glance
- Referred to in the text
- Introduce: present: discuss
- 'Figures': title and decimal number
- Minimum number of words: title, labels, scales, essential information
- Fold-outs for ease of use
- Surround with space on the page

- Landscape format (not portrait)
- Take care with material from other sources
- Beware the law of copyright

Binding and printing

Some reports are printed professionally; some are even designed professionally. In most cases, though, it is the writer who is responsible for binding and printing.

Any binding should be easy to use, hold the pages firmly and look good. There are various kinds available:

- Spiral bindings: allow pages to lie flat for ease of use
- Slide bar: common for internal reports. Cheap but can be awkward and irritating.
- Ring binders are bulky: watch for where the holes will go on the pages.

A cover with a 'window' can be useful and attractive. It will often be available printed with the company logo and might come in a range of colours. Ensure that all the information designed to be seen, is seen: above all, the title and author's name.

Reports to be used in heavy industrial conditions should be produced on grease-resistant paper and bound in wipe-clean covers.

More and more report writers have access to more and more sophisticated word processors, or so-called 'desk-top publishing', which offers far greater versatility in the production of printed material. It is obviously best to know what the machine can – and cannot! – do, before you begin work on the report. Beware of producing a document that looks gimmicky.

Presentation

CHECKLIST 6

- Layout
  - displays the shape of your thoughts
  - consistent throughout report
  - emphasize headings, section and page numbers
  - new page for each section
  - lots of space on the page
  - use lots of lists
- Illustrations
  - relevant; essential to argument?
  - simple: the information at a glance?
  - call them Figures; number; add list to contents
  - fold-outs for ease of use
  - take care to print well
- Binding and printing
  - check available methods
  - use an attractive cover
  - don't be seduced into gimmickry

Checking it over

Revision is a continuous procedure. Checking a long, complex report should not be left until it is complete; it is more accurately and easily carried out as the report is built up.

Checking section-by-section fulfils two functions:

- it eliminates errors and improves the text before revision of the whole draft;
- it keeps the writer's mind focused on the report's purpose.

Typing

If you are not typing the report yourself, be sure to involve the person who is. The typist is potentially your greatest ally in the process of revising and improving the report. Writers only ever see what they think they have written. The typist is invaluable as a fresh and (hopefully!) unbiased eye, able to check the logic of your thoughts, the clarity of your language and the effectiveness of your presentation.

- Involve the typist once the contents page is written. Give a copy of the page to the typist and explain notation and page numbering.
- Ask for comments: is the contents list logical and clear? Ensure that the typist understands all technical terms – and that *you* have spelt them accurately!
- Have each section typed as you go. It is much easier for you to correct a typed first draft; and word processing now allows far easier and quicker revision than in the past.
- Ask the typist to assess each section for overall impact – language and layout.
- The typist should double-check for consistency of spelling, numbers, abbreviations and layout. After all, the typist will be producing the work on the page.
- Include the name of the typist in the report: in the introduction; even on the title page. Why not? Such a strong contribution should not go unrecognized.

Sending each section to be typed before revision has several advantages:

- it enforces a break for the writer before checking;
- the typed draft looks different: more professional;
- errors are far easier to spot on a typescript;
- it involves the typist actively in the construction of the report.

Section Revision

Check and revise each section as it returns from the typist. A good idea is to spend half an hour or so at the beginning of the day, when the mind is clear, checking the previous day's work.

Return to your statement of purpose, and your preparatory notes about the report's reader or user. This is the time to test each section against those initial statements.

CHECKLIST: Daily section revision

- Relevance of material to report's purpose
- Relevance of material to reader's needs/wants
- Logical order of material
- Any material which would be better removed to an appendix: statistics, illustrations, detailed descriptions?
- Headings and sub-headings: accuracy and clarity
- Paragraphs:
  - manageable size
  - topic paragraph at head of section
  - first sentence a summary of each paragraph
  - logically connected

- Sentences:
  - more than 25 words: analyse and reconstruct
  - grammatical errors
  - punctuation
  - readability or awkward expressions
- Words:
  - accurate
  - brief
  - clear
  - spelling
- Layout: margins, spacing; emphasis, highlighting, indenting
- Notation: does it agree with contents page?
- Page numbers: by section (1/1, 1/2 etc.)

Checking the first draft

Once the first draft is completed, a thorough revision of the whole report is possible.

Try to leave as much time as possible between completion of the draft and beginning revision. A week is ideal: 48 hours a reasonable second-best.

First: read from start to finish, in one go. Only in this way will you get a sense of the report's argument and overall impact. Mark any passages requiring attention. Do not stop to deal with them at this point.

Is the report:

- CLEAR?
  - Does it say what you mean it to say? Check against the statement of purpose you produced at the very beginning of the project, and against the reader's requirements. Is the report convincing and persuasive?

- Does it look good? Layout; illustrations; notation; page numbers?
- CONCISE?
  - Have you said it as well as possible? Headings; sub-headings; paragraphs; sentences; words. Repetition? Padding?
- COMPLETE?
  - Is everything there? Is there any crucial information missing or incomplete? Are there any pages missing?
- CORRECT?
  - Are the facts and figures accurate? Do they support your conclusions? Are your recommendations realistic?

Having read from cover to cover, go back to the passages needing adjustment. Once these are dealt with, you can begin the second stage of the revision process: the painstaking work of checking each part of the document.

Discussion with a colleague or superior at this stage can be useful for checking technical content. Helpful and encouraging comments, and positive suggestions for changes, are to be welcomed. A report may of course have to go to a line manager before production to check for confidentiality (or that all-important consideration, 'politics').

The first draft should also be proof-read for typing errors. This is best done by a colleague who has had no connection with the report: another secretary or administrator, perhaps.

Take proof-reading seriously. A single letter mistyped in a health and safety report can be a matter of life and death. Beware the spell-check facility on the word processor: it will not pick up 'there' as an incorrect version of 'their', or 'modern' for 'modem', or 'now' for 'not'. Proof-reading can still only be done by human skill.

Of course, the world being what it is, such luxuries as willing colleagues are not always available: and the final responsibility for revision of the first draft must anyway lie with the writer.

Never revise closely for more than 30 minutes at a time. Use a blank sheet of paper, moved down the page line by line, to help concentration. Tables of figures should be checked by two people, one reading the draft aloud, the other checking from the original.

CHECKLIST: Detailed revision

■ FIRST IMPRESSION: does the report look good?

TITLE PAGE
■ Title: Concise? Specific?
■ Author name(s)?
■ Commissioner or recipient? Job title? Department? Address?
■ Date?
■ Reference number?
■ Confidentiality mark?
■ Copy number?

SUMMARY
■ Brief statement of the report
■ Conclusions, recommendations, action points
■ Can it stand by itself, without the full report?

CONTENTS PAGE
■ Complete?
■ Section headings, sub-headings, as in the text?
■ Notation complete and correct?
■ Page numbers complete and correct?
■ Appendices included?
■ List of illustrations?

INTRODUCTION
- Terms of reference: fully stated?
- Authorizing body or person?
- Objectives: purpose and intended uses of report?
- Methods of investigation and analysis?
- Explanatory statement of arrangement of material?
- Any data which should be in the main body?

FINDINGS
- Purpose: check against statement of purpose. Does the material address it?
- Persuasive?
- Order: logic; hierarchy of main points and sub-points?
- Accuracy: facts and figures?
- Brevity: succinct statements, economical use of words?
- Clarity: Language appropriate to the reader/user?
- Quantity: sufficient data to support the argument? Any section lacking? Anything overlooked? Too much data? Inessential data which could go into an appendix?

CONCLUSIONS
- Natural flow from the findings?
- Itemized?
- Any new data here? If so, remove.
- Every conclusion supported by the data?
- Are they objective? Any unsupported opinions?
- Are they based on additional factors: experience in the field, comparison with similar situations? Are these factors expressed?

RECOMMENDATIONS
- Natural flow from findings and conclusions?
- Itemized? Highlighted?
- Relevant to the terms of reference?
- Appropriate to the situation?
- Do they solve the problem? Or improve the situation?

- A range of possible recommendations: preferred option stated?
- Actions: specific, measurable, achievable? By whom? By when?

APPENDICES

- Are they all there?
- Are they labelled (Appendix A, etc.)
- Are they all necessary?
- Any illustrations which would be better here? Or in the text?
- Glossary and list of abbreviations?
- Differently coloured paper for ease of reference?

ACKNOWLEDGEMENTS

- Complete? In the right place?

REFERENCES AND BIBLIOGRAPHY

- References before bibliography?
- Complete?
- Properly annotated?
  - References: number order (with textual marks);
  - Bibliography: alphabetically.

ILLUSTRATIONS

- All necessary?
- Complete?
- Legible?
- All in their proper place?
- Right illustration for the page?
- Landscape format?
- Statistics: accurate?

LAYOUT

- Consistent throughout report?
- Notation complete and correct?
- New page for each section?
- Sub-sections indented?
- Headings and sub-headings emphasized?

- Wide margins; double spacing?
- All pages numbered?

All this may seem very laborious. It has to be done. Thorough revision is the only way to ensure that no vital aspect of the report is left out.

Remember, too, that reports have a tendency to 'wander': they will almost inevitably by read by people unforeseen by us, either now or in the future. Does the finished report promote our organization as professional, efficient, and caring? Or us, as clear-thinking and decisive?

If the report has been compiled according to the practical, step-by-step procedure outlined in this book, detailed checking will be reasonably straightforward. Once done, it can be handed to the typist to be transformed into the final draft.

The final check

The check of the final draft, before copying and despatch, is a strictly technical matter. Check for:

- Completeness
- Accuracy
- Layout
- Spelling
- Numbers
- Illustrations

Check copies after copying. Photocopiers have been known to miss pages or mysteriously reorder them!

The report is finished. You can hand it over, confident – and proud – that the hard work which you have invested in the project will be handsomely reflected in the finished article.

Checking it over

CHECKLIST 7

- Typing
    - involve typist from the start: include name on title page
    - type each section as you go
- Section revision
    - relevance to purpose and reader
    - accuracy, brevity and clarity throughout
    - layout, notation and page numbers
- Checking the first draft
    - First read, cover to cover: Clear? Concise? Complete? Correct?
    - Proof-read in detail
- The final check
    - for completeness and accuracy

Appendix A

Gunning's Fog Index

For years, educationists and psychologists have sought a means of measuring the readability of a piece of text. Of the many formulae which have been devised, the most celebrated is probably that devised by Gunning in the 1940s.

1. Select a passage of at least 250 words. It must contain full sentences.
2. Count the total number of words in the text. Call this figure 'X'.
3. Count the total number of sentences. Call this figure 'Y'.
4. Calculate the average number of words per sentence: X/Y.
5. Count the number of 'big' words in the text: words with three or more syllables. Call this figure 'Z'. Do not count:

■ proper nouns – the names of people, places, organizations, or products;

- combination words made up of smaller words: *horse-power, catchword, nevertheless,* etc.
- any verb which becomes three or more syllables by the addition of *-es, -ed,* or *ing:* releases, surprising, organizing, motivated, etc.

6. Apply the following formula:

$$[X/Y + (Z/X \times 100)] \times 0.4 =$$

Example

A passage of 231 words has 14 sentences and 28 big words. The average sentence length X/Y is $231/14 = 16.5$. The percentage of big words $(Z/X \times 100)$ is $28/231 \times 100 = 12.1$. The sum of the two $(16.5 + 12.1)$ is 28.6, which multiplied by 0.4 gives a Fog Index of 11.4

Gunning multiplies by 0.4 to give a generally recognized measure of reading age.

What should your Fog Index be?

Index Interpretation

1 – 8   Childish. OK for children or adults with literacy problems. Might offend more capable readers.

8 – 10   Acceptable. Typical of the 'tabloid' press.

10 – 12   Ideal. Suitable for sustained reading by 'typical adults in the general population'.

12 – 14   Acceptable. Typical of the 'quality' press.

14 – 17   Difficult. Typical of academic literature.

17 –   Unreadable.

This is not a scientific analysis of language use. No index can measure sentence structure, thought flow and writing style. Use

Gunning as a *general guide* to the suitability of your writing for various audiences.

Many organizations now subject all their documents to a readability check before publishing.

Appendix B

Writing Numbers

The general rule

Write numbers from one to ten as words; as figures from 10 up.

Most chairs have four legs.
The book contained 134 pages.

Exceptions

- Numbers as words at the beginning of a sentence:
  Fourteen students passed their exams this term.
- Try not to start a sentence with a huge or complicated number!
- Round numbers spelled out as words:
  Some two hundred employees were made redundant.

- Adjoining numbers: spell out the smaller or the first number:
  five 10p pieces;
  three 50ml teaspoons
- Quantities and measurements as figures:
  23 July; Fig.5; 45 Nunhead Grove; 2%
- Ordinal numbers in words, unless in a list:
  the first man on the moon;
  1st prize; 2nd prize; 3rd prize
- Sums of money as figures:
  £467.21; $50; 25p
- Numbers in parallel constructions as figures:
  He bought 3 books, 23 pens,
  7 pencils and 6 packets of paper.

Bibliography

Dictionaries

Chambers English Dictionary, Chambers, 1990
Chambers Concise Dictionary, new edition, Chambers, 1991

The Shorter Oxford English Dictionary, 2 vols., Oxford, 1973
The Concise Oxford Dictionary, 8th ed., Oxford, 1990
The Pocket Oxford Dictionary, 8th ed., Oxford, 1992

Pay your money and take your choice. **The Shorter Oxford English Dictionary** is probably the best affordable dictionary on the market, but its bulk makes it more suitable for the home than for the office.

Roget's Thesaurus, ed. B. Kirkpatrick, Penguin, 1988
The classic 'vocabulary on a large scale, categorized by topics'. Invaluable for discovering new words or recovering forgotten ones.

Guides to grammar and usage

Fowler, H. W., **A Dictionary of Modern English Usage**, 2nd. ed. rev. Sir Ernest Gowers, Oxford, 1965

The most famous guide to English usage. Rather strict and puritanical, but indispensable as the final authority.

Gowers, Sir Ernest, **The Complete Plain Words**, Penguin, 1987

Originally commissioned by the Treasury in 1948, this book has had a profound impact on language use in the Civil Service and beyond. Repeatedly reprinted and often revised, the latest edition includes a useful checklist of words and phrases to be used with care.

Greenbaum, Sidney, **An Introduction to English Grammar**, Longman, 1991

A comprehensive, thoroughly modern survey. Very academic: not for the faint-hearted.

Partridge, Eric, **Usage and Abusage**, Penguin, 1973

A useful companion to Fowler, Partridge is entertaining and full of good sense.

Phythian, B. A., **Teach Yourself English Grammar**, Hodder & Stoughton, 1984

– **Teach Yourself Correct English**, Hodder & Stoughton, 1985

Straightforwrd, approachable guides to grammar and usage, including plenty of exercises and sections on applied writing: reports, letters and so on.

Other books of interest

Buzan, Tony, **Use Your Head**, rev. ed., BBC, 1989

The definitive guide to pattern plans – or, as Buzan calls them, Mind Maps.

van Emden, Joan, and Easteal, Jennifer, **Report Writing**, McGraw-Hill, 1986

The best book I have found on the subject. Rather wordy, and at times a bit fussy, it is nonetheless, comprehensive and practical.

Stanton, Nicki, **Communication**, 2nd. ed., Macmillan, 1990

Includes sections on writing and reports.

A Communication pocket guide

The right report

More reports are being written than ever before. But are they achieving the desired results? Badly written or inaccurate reports not only waste time and effort but can also lead to misinterpretation and reflect badly on the writer.

The right report shows how to write reports and get results. This practical guide is full of simple tips showing how to prepare, gather information, structure the report, how to write accurately and clearly, and how to present the report to its best effect. There is also a chapter on effective checking and appendices include advice on writing numbers and a fog index.

The **Communication pocket guides** form a series of titles on key communication skills. Each title is written by a practising trainer with first hand expertise in the subject. The Society publishes only tried and tested materials which aim to maximise performance and create an environment of best practice at work.

About the author

Alan Barker is an associate adviser with the Communication Skills Department at The Industrial Society. He read English at Cambridge University, and also works in television and radio.

The Industrial Society is the leading authority on best practice in the development of people for and at work. Its principles are aimed quality of management, personal development, involvement at work, creating a learning culture, allowing access and opportunity, productive employee relations and developing links between business, the community and education.

For further information contact:

The Industrial Society

48 Bryanston Square

London W1H 7LN

Tel: 0171 262 2401

£6.95